INQUISITION LANE

Matthew Sweeney

INQUISITION
LANE

BLOODAXE BOOKS

ISBN: 978 1 78037 148 1

First published 2015 by
Bloodaxe Books Ltd,
Eastburn,
South Park,
Hexham,
Northumberland NE46 1BS.

www.bloodaxebooks.com
For further information about Bloodaxe titles
please visit our website or write to
the above address for a catalogue.

Supported using public funding by
**ARTS COUNCIL
ENGLAND**

Cover design: Neil Astley & Pamela Robertson-Pearce.

Printed in Great Britain by Bell & Bain Limited, Glasgow, Scotland, on
acid-free paper sourced from mills with FSC chain of custody certification.

for John Hartley Williams

ACKNOWLEDGEMENTS

Acknowledgements are due to the editors of the following publications where some of these poems first appeared: *The Atlanta Review*, *The Chattahoochie Review*, *Cyphers*, *The Dark Horse*, *The Edinburgh Review*, *The Irish Times*, *The London Review of Books*, *The Malpais Review*, *New Walk*, *The North*, *The Pickled Body*, *Ploughshares*, *Poetry*, *Poetry Ireland Review*, *Poetry London*, *Poetry Review*, *Southword*, *The Rialto*, *Riddlefence*, *The Same*, *The Spectator*, *The Stinging Fly*, *Stand*, *The Warwick Review*, and *The Wolf*.

A few of the poems were first included in the following small publications: *The Gomera Notebook* (Shoestring Press, 2014) and *Twentyone Men and a Ghost* (The Poetry Business, 2014).

'Co-Author' was printed in a handset limited edition by the Bonnefant Press / Banholt in 2014.

'Benito' was awarded third prize in the 2013 Gregory O'Donoghue Competition.

CONTENTS

11 The Dream House
12 The Devil's Castle
13 The One-eyed Philosopher of Katmandu
14 The Crow
15 Benito
16 The Igloo
17 Cat Burial
18 Circus
20 The Poem You've Been Waiting For
21 Do Wah Diddy Diddy Do
22 The Indian
23 The Biggest Task
25 A Calf in the English Market
27 The Beauty Institute
28 New York
32 The Twins
33 The Canary
34 Guns
36 Driving to Sabratha
35 Greenland
38 The Insurance Agent
39 The Matador
40 Toro
41 Poem
42 Bouncing
43 Blue in the Tiergarten
44 Catholicism in Germany
45 Gold
46 Into the Air
47 Cloud Communication
48 Elegy for the Moonman
50 Inquisition Lane
51 The Other Bible

53 The Periscope
54 The First Lighthouse Keeper
55 The Mallow Races
56 The Rock
57 Ice Sculpture
58 Doll
59 The Big Umbrella
60 The Archery Lesson
62 San Francisco
66 Trainsong
68 Green Sky
69 The Gare du Nord
70 The Chocolate Mine
72 The Dead Zone
73 The Visited Man
74 The Dog and the Moon
75 Broken Flower
77 Muskerry Villas: A Diptych
79 Creature Haiku
80 Hogs Killing a Snake
81 The Gallows
82 The Loop
83 The Stomp
84 My Problem
85 I Don't Want to Get Old
86 The Sneezer
87 The Ghost
88 Co-Author

95 *Biographical note*

Tis the middle of Night by the Castle Clock,
And the Owls have awaken'd the crowing Cock:
    Tu-u-whoo! Tu-u-whoo!
And hark, again! The crowing Cock,
How drowsily it crew.

SAMUEL TAYLOR COLERIDGE

The Dream House

The dream house was yellow
and had no chimneys. Its one
window was round, a porthole
so big a child could stand in it.
The door was smaller, and red,
with a golden chain and padlock.

Around the house was a Zen
garden of sand raked in circles,
with occasional bonsai palmtrees,
each with its own yellow spider
swaying on its gossamer web.

Behind the house was a long,
flat mountain that sloped left.
White goats could be seen on it,
and a few climbers, or walkers –
the gradient being so gentle.

Inside the house was a circular
staircase with yellow mosaics
leading to the inner, upper haven.
There was no furniture downstairs.
There was no one living there.

The Devil's Castle

is white, to fool everyone who
stumbles upon it, and the doors
are green. A parrot is the sentry
and he's fluent in fifty languages.
The smell of goat curry seeps out
from the kitchen that's staffed by
blind chefs, and a bald vintner
waves half a dozen bottles of
local *premier cru* at the arriver.
It would be a churl who'd decline.

It would be a genius who'd know
what to say there. 'Where have I
landed? Who is the good sir here'?
I think not. I'd opt for the silence
of the moon, the stare of the sun.
I'd get out of there as soon as I
knew where I was. I'd leave hungry,
thirsty. I'd hitchhike back to the
harbour and take a boat to Limbo.
I'd keep looking after me, though.

The One-eyed Philosopher of Katmandu

The more a man wants, the less he gets –
so said the One-eyed Philosopher of Katmandu
over hot goats' urine and baked goat turds

that spring day I bumped my mountain-bike
up those steep, twisty roads to his green hut
camouflaged with lurid, sticky green creepers.

A bespectacled parrot was his sole companion,
and it chanted at regular intervals: *Death comes
to those fools who are never expecting him.*

The philosopher took out his glass eye to rub,
then replaced it in its socket. Typical of a bird,
he said, to be so sure of great death's gender.

I myself, he continued, know nothing about it,
beyond the fact it's a clifftop, and we all must
take the bewildering step off the edge into space.

And you, my young poet, he said, addressing me –
Be sure in your scribing to speak of that space
and nothing else, and then you may get everything.

The Crow

Among those gathered at the grave
were the two murderers, neither of
whom were known or recognised

except by the crow who'd sat in a tree
above the corner of the field where
the two had stabbed and stabbed

the tall young farmer who'd dared to
refuse to sell his family's century-old
farmhold to the big city development

that had plans to build a round hotel.
The crow watched from a tombstone
one villain whispering to the other

while the priest swung the thurible
over the black coffin, chanting prayers
as a woman and two children cried,

then the bird cawed loudly and flew
at the first murderer, pecking his face
till blood splattered his pointy shoes

whereupon the second thug felt a
beak gouge out an eye, and pain such
as he never believed he'd experience.

At that the crow rose into the air, flew
in a circle over the two fallen assassins
and left them to the appalled crowd.

Benito

Benito, I remember you jumping
into the river, with your clothes on,
trying to catch the otter. I had to hold
out a broken branch to save you, then
gather more and light them, so
you could dry out. We slept there
on the riverbank, helped by the
brandy we were slugging, sniffed at,
no doubt, by water rats and stoats,
but only after you woke the forest-
creatures with your baritone. You
hadn't a bad voice, Benito, though
you failed all your auditions –
you even got me joining in. Then,
in the morning, you climbed a tree,
to pee from a height into the river.
It cleared your head, you said,
and you caught trout with your hands
to spear on twigs and roast for
breakfast, demanding an espresso,
which I provided in the border station.

The Igloo

Outside the igloo he waited
for an invitation to come inside.
There was no knocker, no doorbell.
He coughed, there was no reply.

He crouched down and peered in.
He felt the warm air from a fire
pat his cheeks and ruffle his hair.
Hello he said quietly and repeated it.

The frost in his toes urged him in,
so did the pain in his gut. His knees
one by one welcomed the snow
and brought him into the warmth.

He stood up and breathed deeply.
He held a foot up to the flames
then swapped it for the other foot.
He lay down on the polar bear rug

but a smell yanked him upright again
and led him to a dresser of bone
where a bowl sat with a cover on it.
He lifted this to reveal dried meat.

He grabbed a chunk and tore at it
with his teeth. It was reindeer.
He devoured all that was in the bowl
and went looking for some more.

He found none, but there was a bottle
of firewater which he swigged.
He swigged again and left it down.
He lay on the bearskin and fell asleep.

Cat Burial

Above the hole in the ground, an oak
dropped leafy branches, between which
I had to duck, to throw in the dead cat,
then spoon back all the dug-out earth.

I'd picked that site because the beast
had sat in the tree, hoping to claw small
birds down to the ground, to devour.
She'd never managed to do so once,

but each time one feathered creature
swooped down, she uttered a weird cry
and swiped at the air, always missing.
I used to stand there, laughing at her,

which earned me a glower and a hiss,
a hunched back, and a wagging tail,
after which she'd leap down and run
into the kitchen, to lie there and yowl.

Once, I remember, she was confronted
by a rat, but turned and ran. I understood,
and told her so – and earned a scratch.
Still, I'd sometimes feed her anchovies.

She'd rarely pass beyond my garden
but this last time she did, and nibbled
meat laced with rat-poison. I found her
feet up, in the dried pond, ridiculous.

I tried to blame the Scottish neighbour
but nothing sticks here. Acts of God,
or of the Devil. Anyway, she's gone now –
subsumed beneath her favourite tree.

Circus

The dog walked the tightrope
with a yellow bow round his neck
and a red top hat on his head .

He was followed by a monkey
on a unicycle. This hairy fellow
wore a luminous green jockstrap.

And close behind, came a Siamese
cat wearing purple shades, and a
purple silk scarf tied to her tail.

This was nothing to the baby
alligator who sashayed across
the rope wearing a blue waistcoat

or the hedgehog with the gold
bandana who slowly edged his
way to the other side, causing

gasps to leave the audience
who were hugely appreciative
of all these animal performers

but who began booing, when a
boy in a white tracksuit pranced
out onto the rope, twirling a stick.

An apple was thrown. Obscene
words were shouted. The boy
paid no attention, did a dance

(including a somersault) in the
middle of the rope, farted loudly,
threw his stick into the audience,

sent his grin round the tent,
and jumped, shrieking, into the
arms of the waiting gorilla.

The Poem You've Been Waiting For

This is the poem you've been waiting for –
me too – and in it I have a blind dog
walking alongside a slithering rattlesnake
on North Main Street in Cork, where
Romanian gypsies in long skirts walk by
in groups, and Auntie Nellie's sweetshop
tempts. Yes, the blind dog and the snake –
I look after them, of course, and lead them

down to the river. People try to stop us – boys
with girls, in particular, but I ignore them.
I sit cross-legged on the pedestrian bridge
at the end of the Grand Parade, with the two
chaps beside me, and people throw coins
which I leave behind me as we walk away.
No one pays attention in Douglas Street,
so we march on to the end, then ignore

the instruction to remain in the south.
Instead, we hail a taxi; within which the
blind dog, the rattlesnake, and I, venture
back to Sunday's Well, to the genteel,
dog-fouled slopes, the butcher with a hat,
and I let the dog and the snake free to
gambol along the pavement, while I
roam behind them, absolutely on guard.

Do Wah Diddy Diddy Do

Singing *Do Wah Diddy Diddy Do*
I jumped off the white shaky bridge
into the River Lee, and swam back-
stroke towards town, past the closed-
down fancy hotel, with the red walls
of the old asylum looming up above
on the opposite bank, and a heron
eyed me from where he stood on one
leg in the shallow water – he clearly
didn't like my song so I sang louder
till he rose and flew away, circling
over me as if he couldn't believe me.

Do Wah Diddy Diddy Do I roared
at a kayak that passed, earning me
a German expletive I replied to in
kind, barely disturbing the song's
rhythm, then I veered left as the river
split, preferring to swim in the shade,
wishing I'd brought along a banana
tucked in my soggy pocket – the peel
would have floated and fed some gulls
and they would have liked my song,
then I climbed out, dripping, at the
Opera House, and I stopped singing.

The Indian

He sat on the mule, slumped forward.
They'd tied him into the saddle
and whacked the beast down the hill
to the cabin on the lake, with the blue
light above the door like a pet star
that knew him well and waited for him.
Oh, he was looked after, that madman.

The snake he'd caught and tethered
to the gate was very poisonous.
He left no sign pointing this out, nor
did he mention that the albatross he'd
caught in a net and freed in the cellar
was vicious. He never underlined.
Let things happen as they were wont to.

At the cabin, his wolf welcomed him
by howling, and when he was released
from the mule by his muttering lover
who helped him over the threshold,
he smiled, and kissed her, earning
a slap, then wobbled into the kitchen
to find the bottle of Mescal, and he

remembered, in a previous life, being
a pre-hispanic Indian in Monte Albán.
Yes, he did, then collapsed asleep
on the floor, to dream of his murder
at the hands of a Spanish conquistador.
He woke from this with a great thirst,
but no sore head, and he drank water.

The Biggest Task

Thinking of the tasks awaiting me,
I thought I'd begin with the biggest –
the burial of the elephant, admittedly
a calf, though bigger and heavier
than a pig. I flapped one huge ear,
then the other, remembering Wally's
skill with a football, dribbling it
through the feet of the laughing boys,
trumpeting when he scored a goal.
And the way he'd let the dog ride him,
barking as they gathered speed, down
the hill to the sea where they'd splash in.

Who would have wanted to poison him?
The film crews that arrived at the gate,
begging to film him; the lady poet
who hung around the house, scribbling
in her notebook, clearly at work on an epic;
or the sculptor moulding his soft lead –
weigh all these against his murderer.
Where was the singer with his protest song,
or the eco-terrorist who'd revenge him?
Why did the police not even believe me?
I was surprised the gentlemen in white
weren't sent to put a tight coat on me.

I decided it had to be the strand, the far
end, near the ruined castle. I hired
a digger and its driver, who lifted
poor Wally into my trailer, and the boys
came to say goodbye to him, as did
a crowd that gathered, including a piper
who sounded a slow air. We dug a hole

and pushed him in, then covered him.
The boys laid a circle of stones on top,
then we stood around till the tide
rolled in. I went home to my *Talisker*.
The rest of my tasks could bloody wait.

A Calf in the English Market

(for Kay Harte)

A calf walked into the English Market
and tripped along past the meat stalls
without even as much as a quiet moo.

He stopped at the Organic Garden to
gobble a small head of lettuce, while
the woman in charge clapped him on.

The smell of freshly brewed coffee was
a new one to him, and he didn't like it,
but he loved all the Pig's Back cheeses

and strained his head up to the counter
till the Spanish assistant leaned over
to put a chunk of Gruyère in his mouth.

Chewing thoroughly, he veered down
to the fish stalls but the laid-out fruit
of the sea sent him trotting away, tail

swishing, till he came to the crooked
staircase and clambered up and round
the corner, lured by the smell of custard,

and nearly knocked down a waitress
carrying a bowl of it with a slice of apple
tart underneath. She recovered, smiled

and left the bowl on the ground for the
visitor to lick clean, then lie down for a
sleep, only to be woken by the choral

shriek that greeted the youthful butcher
who'd followed the calf with a stun-gun
and a cleaver, and now fled downstairs.

The Beauty Institute

The Beauty Institute was closed
so I went to the harbour, where
boys in blue were trying to toss
boys in red into the water, with
the aid of wooden lances, while
Arab music tootled along. I myself

was lacking in instruction, so I sat
in a bar on the Corniche with a beer,
composing a curse for the editor
who'd dropped me. I forced myself
to encompass this in a sestina,
a form I knew he hated, but as

a wet blueboy was fished out of
the churning water, I found my
sestina being derailed by beauty,
the concept of it. What was it?
These boys in their coloured hoops?
Their girlfriends clapping them?

Brassens' echoes on the waters?
Monet's water lilies in Giverny?
A poodle dancing on the table
in *Chez Jacques*, where the grilled
squid goes well with a carafe of *Picpoul*?
A bald baby crawling under it?

It was too much, too big a subject.
I tore the page out of the notebook,
scrunched it into a ball and chucked
it into the water, then headed up
the high road to a view of the sea,
and the soothing *Cimetière Marin*.

New York

1

I kept glimpsing Lou
Reed's ghost as I roamed
Manhattan – there he
was on street corners,
in every sportsbar. I
heard snatches of his
songs on the urban wind.
It was the middle of
a perfect, perfect day.

2

If only time machines
weren't so expensive,
or had such side-effects,
I'd go back to drink red
wine with Frank O'Hara –
I'm sure we'd find one
we both liked. I'm less
sure he'd like this, but
there's always a chance.

3

At MOMA I stood for
ages in front of Magritte's
Daring Sleeper, the baldie
under the brown blanket
in the tigerskin-patterned
box, the apple, candle,
bird, blue bow, hairbrush,
hand-mirror embedded in
the higgledy-piggledy grave-
stone before the overcast sky.
I stared, remembering it all.

4

I tried to take a taxi to the
Chelsea Hotel but the cabbie
went on a wide detour in
bad traffic, and when I saw
I was back in Midtown, I
hopped out and slunk off
to my small, unsung hotel.

5

In West Village a pair of
bums approached – one with
a wilted flower in his button-
hole. They watched a long,
black car pull in, allowing
the driver to jump out and
buy an apple. I heard
one bum say to the other
Oh, man, there's our limo.

6

In Bleecker Street I found
the world's best cheese-
shop (well, the oldest in
New York) and coolest
Italian deli, and I bought
designer pasta, then took
my red eye and sore toe to
the Slaughtered Lamb pub.

7

On West 4th Street I had
a hell of nerve, and stood
in front of Dylan's old flat,
where he invited someone to
please crawl out her window.

Yeah... I wanted to photo-
graph it but a sex-shop
downstairs intervened.

8

At the side of Washington
Square was the dog-run.
From all sides dogs on leads
made for it, to be set free
and allowed to run in packs,
barking – except for the Afghan
who sat on the bench with his
mistress, observing everything.

9

In Union Square's Farmers'
Market, I drank goat's-milk
yoghurt, then followed closely
three chess games on the street-
side. I'd have lost each one.

10

In a Mexican Restaurant
in East Village I ate monkfish
with molé and fried, green
bananas, also slow-roasted
pork with green sauce. I drank
three margaritas, and some
Argentinian red wine.
A sombrero floated down
and landed on my head.

11

Back in Hell's Kitchen I
wandered down 9th Avenue
to Petland, and bought a
frondy thing for Derek, my
goldfish, then crossed to the
Amish deli for watermelon juice.

12

In JFK's Security, where the
black guys in uniform made me
laugh, I launched five plastic
trays through the screener –
one with my boots, one my
belt and jacket, and bag of
little bottles, one my new
mini iPad, the last two with
my rucksacks, big and small.

The Twins

are far from identical. One is half-blind,
the other hunts small birds with a crossbow.

One has a decent tenor voice, the other
rasps out the obituaries on local radio.

One is vegan, the other eats everything,
and his favourite meat is bush rat, which

he frequents African restaurants to ingest.
His brother fails to accompany him there.

What have they in common? Blond hair,
a liking for horseracing, and the curious songs

of Leonard Cohen. Did they have the same
mother? Decidely, yes. The same father?

Of course! Get real. Ask one what his favourite
film is, the other will answer *Twin Peaks*

even though it was a series, and not a film.
They once nearly died in a fire, but one

saved the other. Which is their mother's pet?
She won't tell you. Their father says he should

sell them to an animal-free zoo, but no one
at all believes him, least of all the twins.

The Canary

A canary in a cage sang to me
as I walked through the market.

I stopped. It sang louder,
so loud I thought its yellow body

would burst. I touched a bar
of the cage. The canary went quiet,

raised one foot and observed me,
then began singing again –

a much happier tune this time.
I knew I had to buy it, and

after a bit of haggling in Arabic,
of which I knew one word,

I emerged, holding the cage.
The canary sang an aria.

We were followed by feral cats.
Passers-by stared at me.

There was the problem of the plane –
how could I get that cage on?

The canary was tiny. If I dumped
the cage, it would fit in my pocket.

I could tie its beak shut, although
I wanted it to keep singing.

Anyway, I'd meditate in the hotel.
Then I'd know what to do.

Guns

'Everyone here has a gun now'
the taxi driver said, 'And
the crime rate is down.' We
were leaving the old city in
Tripoli – those alleys and bazaars
teeming with people, with
cheap jewellery (mainly gold,
or what looked like gold), scarves,
jackets, teeshirts, even Arab three-
piece-suits; with antique knives,
suitcases, ornamental lamps,
and always, in the quieter alleys,
men sitting on outside chairs.
While we waited for the stragglers
to catch up, a small boy ran to
us with a toy rifle in his hands
and pretended to shoot someone
who pretended to die. Later,
a young man in camouflage uniform
bustled by, unarmed, and I
remembered the bullet holes I'd seen
on arrival from the airport,
the wrecked cars pushed off the
roads, the bombed walls
of Gadaffi's compound, all the
manifestations of the country's
new flag (that was the old flag),
flapping everywhere, and printed
on the caps of returning young
men on the plane, the murals
announcing in Arabic and English
that Libya was free. Later
that evening, after the reading,

we went to a restaurant
to share a Turkish meal. Half-
way through we were startled by
the rat-tat-tat of machine guns.
'Youths with AK 47s,' our host said.
'They love firing into the air.'

Driving to Sabratha

I woke with a nose bleed
then we headed off in the minibus
to Sabratha. On the way
we passed a graffiti-daubed tank
parked at the side of the road.
Then came a blown-up villa.
There were bullet holes in the walls
of the houses in the long, strung-
out town we drove through,
and most of these were abandoned.
Red scaffolding cradled the tower
of the mosque. Leaving town
we saw a string of artisans'
ornate, metal doors, then
a flock of small, dirty sheep
on the grass verge, with one goat
amidst them, and traffic stopped
in the other lane, because of
broken eggs all over the road.
The machine gun in the pickup truck
had tarpaulin over it. The roadblock
was offduty. The minibus pulled
into a track and we saw the looming
ruins of the Roman city of Sabratha,
spread out against the sea.

Greenland

And maybe I'll go online
and book a flight to Nuuq,
to eat seals' eyeballs
deep-fried in blubber,
or seals' noses, also
deep-fried, their whiskers
stiff as toothpicks. I'll swig
the local firewater, and sing
Irish songs – expatriate ones,
Lord Franklin, or maybe
The Coast of Malabar, even
if the geography's wrong.

And if the locals threaten
me, saying my voice is shite,
my songs an abomination,
I'll pull out an old Irish jersey
signed by Roy Keane, and I'll
ask them what colour it is,
and what land they'd come to
if they stepped into the sea
and kept walking – south, of
course – to emerge in Donegal,
and what if a pair of pipers
greeted them on the shore?

The Insurance Agent

He rode along sideways, two feet
hanging down the same side of the white
mare who held her head high, as she
trotted through the cactus-filled valley,
where sidewinders slithered underhoof.

An ambitious vulture hovered overhead.
A coyote howled in the distance. He
ignored them both, and pulled out a
stick of chorizo which he gnawed on,
while letting his binoculars show him

what lay ahead. It was a crashed plane
spread out there in the desert, seats,
bodies thrown everywhere (although
bones would better describe the last),
and the sun glinted off its fuselage.

He dismounted, took out his notebook,
walked around, turning over the half-
devoured corpses and making entries,
till he had enough, then he got back on
the mare, a leg each side this time.

The Matador

The matador scowled at the back
of the bar, and sipped his beer.
He wanted to stab the people
who stared at him. His black tie,
his black suit didn't shield him
from their eyes. He ordered
testicles, his unique entitlement,
and a carafe of deep red wine.
He flung his right arm around,
as if he was twirling his cape,
and declaimed a line of poetry,
then giggled, and apologised.
Tomorrow he was going out
against a bull from Miura. Where
was the flashbulb reception?
He fixed his eyes on a bearded
man who might be discussing him –
He sipped his wine, remembering
the white-socked bull in Toledo.
He could never be defeated.

Toro

I'm the only bull who was set free.
I gambol round the field all day,
I have both my ears and my tail.
The matador recalls me with a shudder.

I came very close to goring him,
closer to one of his banderilleros
who was carried off with a bloodied
leg, and walks now with a limp.

I hoofed the ground, looked up,
snorted, then charged at the matador.
I shook the darts from my back,
made sure to keep my shoulders closed.

I ripped his suit of lights, knocked
the sword from his hand. I chased him
to the wooden perimeter which he
vaulted over. I waited for him

and he came back, stood angled,
held out his red cape which I
tossed aside, then swivelled to try
to nail him this final time. It was

not to be. The handkerchiefs waved,
the President signalled it over. The
matador looked at me and bowed.
I muscled round the sandy ring

with the crowd on their feet, yelling,
clapping, and loud music playing.
Hundreds of flashbulbs went off.
I ate the best grass that evening.

Poem

After the weekend, I climbed the hill
above the castle and shot a hare that
I skinned by torchlight and marinated
in garlic, fresh thyme, and red wine,
after severing it with my sharp knife
that I keep for the special occasions.

An owl sat on the windowsill, staring
till I shooed it away. I put on music –
a new country songwriter, steeped
in blood. The choruses spiralled out.
I opened recently-acquired brandy, and
began to sketch a portrait of myself.

I soon began to resemble a monster,
one with tiny red ears, and spiky hair,
and a nose befitting a renegade goblin .
I needed to change the music, so I opted
for Tom Waits this time, *Bone Machine*,
which went much farther than blood.

I went out to the garden to pick oregano,
chopped it, and added it to the hare.
I should have thought of this earlier.
Who should I invite to dinner tomorrow?
I put my unlicensed gun back in its drawer,
and covered it with my underwear.

Bouncing

Bouncing on the trampoline, he saw
the visible slice of his world changing
but only temporarily. The Italian jazz
he had on *loud* helped this only so
much. He ordered his terrier, Judas,
to join him up there but the dog barked,
gurned, and lay down, watching him.
He was on his own in his bouncing.

A trumpet twirl made him try a leap
that plunged him onto the carpet.
Judas was on top of him, licking his
face. Even the cat, Valmina, investigated,
but bade a haughty retreat. He rose,
climbed back on the trampoline, and
bounced with complete abandon.
A tall table lamp fell to the ground.

After ten minutes of this, he paused
for a glass of red wine, then another.
Judas laid a head on his lap, and he
stroked him, then rejoined the trampoline
to bounce some more, yodelling this
time, flinging his arms out, like a prima
donna, swaying this way and that. His
world was the same when he stopped.

Blue in the Tiergarten

(for Dr K)

One man slept on the grass,
one on a bench. A third sat
awake, with his dog asleep
beside him. Then came the blue
square on the trunk of a tree,
and a sign forbidding ballgames.
Pleasure boats waited on the Spree
to fill with tourists, while joggers
whizzed past in reds and yellows.
I sat on a bench to rest, watching
one swan caress another, while a
woman broke off bits of a baguette
to feed them. The blue square –
what did it signify? If I'd traversed
every metre of the Tiergarten
would I have encountered others?
Was an artist obsessed with blue,
and with the shape of the square?
I immediately wanted to copy him
or her, and paint squares of
the exact same shade of blue
on every tree in the Tiergarten,
till all the joggers wore blue,
the boats were resprayed blue,
the leaves grew out blue, and
the sleepers woke up, smiling.

Catholicism in Germany

A monk on a motorbike flashed by
as I walked down Kantstrasse. I'd eaten
a Chinese lunch – duck with mushrooms
and beansprouts – and drunk a *Weisser
Burgunder*, and was bound for a siesta.
All this was derailed by the monk.

Then a second monk farted my way
with a nun on the pillion. What was
happening to Catholicism in Germany?
Three more monks revved past me
(two with nuns) and I twigged
they were all on Harley-Davidsons.

The sheen on their steeds was like
stars on the Wannsee. Their habits
were designed by Versace. I stood
to watch the host of them vanish –
at least a hundred in all – and after
them the long Kantstrasse was empty.

Gold

After the murder, I called a meeting
to see if we were happy. I declared
I was not – I said I liked the man
we shot. You all disagreed with this.
I asked if you knew him, his wife,
none of you did. 'Kill me, then,
I said.' They all stared at me. 'Why,
Bernard? Of course we won't.'
'Why not?' I said. 'He was a good
man, a better man than me. And
look at what I've brought you –
rubbish, dodgy tales, dross.'
'Easy to dismiss that,' you said.
'We appreciated it all. And you
wandered the wild paths to bring
it back to us – your songs, your
legends, magic stories, your gold.'
I thanked you, but shook my head.
The good man was dead. I didn't care
What I'd brought you. I needed to go.
I packed up my sagas, my song lyrics,
my alchemy potions, my gold, and
I disappeared.

Into the Air

(i.m. Seamus Heaney)

I think I'll forget the concelebrated mass
around your coffin, the way those priests
claimed you as a starry one of their own,

and the high choral singing, meant to lead
you through the diamond-studded gates
of heaven, where you'd sign books for God.

I'll forget, too, the way that crow of a bishop
had to have the last word by croaking out
some blasted Latin hymn (although

you liked Latin) straight after your piper
played an unearthly slow air to guide your
coffin down into that hole in the ground in

Bellaghy, your own place, where, two
nights later a harpist was found playing to you
in the dark, as if you'd invited her there

to set everything right. I'll remember that,
and the piper's lament, and your Derry voice,
and your laugh, and yes, maybe a poem or two.

Cloud Communication

(i.m. Dennis O'Driscoll)

You sent me several emails, but I can only find one.
In it you talk about swimming horses, and loaned books
that never come back. You say you won't lend again.

I want to receive another email from you, one that
tells me about where you are. Is Yeats with you?
Is he as mad and pompous as we imagine he'd be?

If you like I won't reply to you. You once told me
that all poets had a word that was key to them,
and that mine was 'border'. I won't take chances.

You could use a pseudonym and come in by junk mail.
You could write it in German – I know you loved Brecht.
You could insert weird fluttery angels and mermaids –

anything quirky to alert me that it's coming from you.
I promise I'll be on the look-out from now. I don't
expect any more of your legendary handwritten cards.

When I read again in Dublin, (if I'm invited back),
I wouldn't mind seeing you there in the audience
clutching a book I've yet to publish that I should sign.

Dennis, let's keep our communication electronic.
I know you weren't too comfortable with this, but
it's our simplest option now. You can attach the odd

posthumous poem (I promise I'll keep it to myself),
and I'd love if you added an audio recording, though I know
this is pushing it. I'd just love to have an email from you.

Elegy for the Moonman

Oh, Neil Armstrong, I met you
in Shropshire, in some arts retreat.
I was there on a college project.
You were on tour, giving talks
about your dance on the moon.
I never heard you, too busy drinking
and playing table-tennis so fiercely
I concussed myself on a metal pipe.
Next morning I had to leave the
lecture to puke. I went to the bar
for a water, and there you were
on a barstool, sipping pink gin.

You smiled, asked who I was, then
said you were Neil Armstrong, the
moonman. I sat and you told me all
about the moon, but first you asked
if I could drive. I couldn't, and you
laughed, advising me to learn to fly
first, as you did. And you flew far.
When you took the Eagle down to
the Tranquil Sea, what were you
thinking? You sat there for hours
before descending to bounce on
the moon, with Buzz bouncing too.

You ordered another gin, got me
a second water, then darkened
and said *The moon fucked me up,*
it fucked up all of us who walked
on it, looking back at that blue ball.
How do you think it feels to be so
far away? When I got home I wanted

to return there, but I knew I never would. It kept some of me, though. I'm really up there still, and when I die my ghost will fly to my foot-prints, and I'll haunt the moon.

Inquisition Lane

Last night I walked down Inquisition Lane
to the bank of the Guadalquivir. I'd eaten

fried chicken with garlic, grilled lambs' kidneys,
and drunk a bottle of Ramon Bilbao Rioja Crianza.

No one had tortured me for my lack of faith
in the gilted Madonna or the cross-carrying Christ.

No one was going to throw me in the river,
minus my thumbs, fingers or testicles.

I'd even watched Barcelona win in silence,
they were as popular as Protestants in Seville.

Inquisition Lane was dim but not dark –
the moon hung low above it, and swallows

darted about, over my long-haired head.
I heard the faint sound of flamenco singing.

I reached the river, and saw a boat there –
without thinking I jumped in. The oars

moved through the water by themselves
and brought me to Inquisition Castle

which had reassembled itself on the riverbank
and welcomed me into its dark basement.

The Other Bible

It took them until 2073 to meet us,
to land in a flurry of flashing lights
on the outskirts of Adelaide, their
cruciform-shaped craft glowing
lemon yellow, and emitting a low
music that brought dogs barking.

The police arrived too, blaring and
shouting into phones that the army
must come. They ordered us all
to keep our distance, but the dogs
ignored this and stood around,
whimpering, till a door opened.

I inched forward but was pushed
back. I was still one of the closest
to the two tall figures who emerged –
giraffe tall, with dog faces – and
the silence around us was celestial.
Even the police became Zen monks.

So smart of them not to choose
America, I reflected, and a firm
thought-command drew me forward,
the police backing away, till I stood
in front of the two tall figures,
hand held out, but they ignored this.

Instead, tendons came from their
bellies which curled round my head,
and they thought-spoke to me in
unison, saying they came in peace
from planet *Illyos*. I glanced around
and verbalised a welcome, which was

echoed loudly. Then they conveyed
to me they wanted to present an
offering, and something very like
a book, in a fantastic edition, came
floating out of the craft, and one of
the two directed it into my hands.

Hieroglyphs, was what occurred to me,
picture stories, weird, futuristic ones –
a tall dog-faced figure with a yellow
cruciform glowing above his head,
flying through space, hauling a horde
of airborne devotees to a yellow valley

in a pleasant world that wasn't ours –
it had above it a faint lavender sky.
I saw no more, except it was their past.
They registered this, re-entered their
craft, which glowed yellow, and took
off as three army vehicles whizzed up.

The Periscope

Up on the roof, he saw the periscope
poking out of the sea. He shouted he
wanted binoculars, but they laughed.

His brother reminded him he was up
there to get the picture back on the tv.
His father said the U-boats were over.

But the curled top of the periscope kept
his attention, so much so that he left
the aerial and climbed down the ladder

and legged it to the beach, the dog, Shay,
running, barking beside him. Roars and
objections came on the wind behind him.

A cow came to the barbed wire to give
a nosy moo, as he loped by, whistling.
A crow flew low over his head, cawing.

There was no one on the beach, except
a longhaired meditator, humming and
bowing in rhythm, so he marched on to

his favourite rock which he climbed
and sat on, staring out at the sea. Shay lay,
whimpering. The periscope was big now.

Soon the submarine would surface, and
he would rush down to embrace the sailors,
offering himself as their long-lost soulmate.

The First Lighthouse Keeper

I was the first lighthouse keeper on Inishtrahull.
I switched on the light for the Prince Regent
in February 1813 – he came in on a flag-fluttering
frigate of the Royal Navy, and docked at the pier
on the east side of the island where the tower rose
and where I was now lord of the darkened waves.

No ships bound for Derry would now founder
on invisible rocks. No uniform was neater than
mine. The hundredweights of coal my men carried
up those windy stairs to fuel the light that dazzled
the night would have sufficed to build a coal castle.
I have to admit I hardly slept at all that first year.

From the beginning we had an Argand lamp, and
a Fresnal lens. There was no better-equipped light-
house down the whole long, stringy coast of Ireland.
I was loved by London – they even permitted me
to keep a pet seal, contrary to strict regulations.
I took to calling the slippery fellow Lumen Meum.

At sixty I permitted myself to sit down and pen my
memoirs. My herb garden was by then legendary,
and I'd published the well-received *Inishtrahull
Cookbook*. My seal was buried in the graveyard,
despite objections. My successor had already
been appointed. I wished the poor fellow well.

The Mallow Races

Have you ever been to the Mallow Races?
It takes some doing as they don't exist.
Try finding them online, or in the *Racing Post*,
and you'll think you're among the dead.
But if you proceed to Cork's Kent Station
a train to Mallow awaits to bring you to
the old sugar town, where a free shuttle
bus whisks you to the racetrack, and you
step out in full view of the horseboxes
to join the meeting officially called Cork.
Why this name-change? I've no idea, but
you've no time to bother with that stuff.
You have a racecard to purchase, and go
through, over a quick coffee, then
proceed to the parade ground to watch
the horses from the first race walk around.
Take note of that grey and white filly, or
that huge black racing machine in her wake.
Now it's over to the phalanx of bookies
to find the best price for your chosen horse,
then do the little secret dance in the toilet
chanting out the nag's name in a whisper.
And if you have a big win (I hope you do),
please come looking for me. I'll be the man
with the blond moustache and yellow shirt
giving out tips in the bar. I'll expect a drink.

The Rock

Maybe there's a rock – no, a very small island
with a cave on it, that we could land our raft on,
and run with the seeds to plant vegetables.
The hope of one small tree would be too much

but there might be some edible tiny creatures,
some maritime, some not, and wild samphire –
and, leaving the foodstuff aside, butterflies,
crow-cousins, puffins, multicoloured jellyfish,

and maybe even bees, with their wild honey
(see, the food is back!) that we'd have to steal,
though we'd have forgotten to bring wheat-seeds
and couldn't return for them now. Still, perhaps

some seeds of the island grass could be ground
between big pebbles, and a kind of unleavened
bread might be slowly baked in stone ovens,
overseen by a half-naked, barefoot hopping me.

I'd like also, ideally, to find banks of coloured clay
to finally try to be a painter, using my fingers,
of course, and I'd endeavour to sketch picture
after picture of you all over the walls of the cave.

Ice Sculpture

If I begged you to, would you hitchhike
to the ice-sculpture factory, where
the drunken cow was just presented,
and the sleeping horse was celebrated.
Ah, those caught animals, where else
would they be paraded? I visualise you
sitting on a black camel, wearing a red
fedora, and a maroon, velvet dress.

It would be sunset, rosé wine would be
flowing, the monkey would be dancing
to zither music. I picture you laughing,
then directing the singing to include a
hymn to a snail, that small fellow who
brings his home with him – easily shown
in ice. And maybe an encore to a frog
who sits on a plate, waiting to dance.

Doll

You're my all-time doll, you're my hedgehog;
You're my missing *Steinpilz*, you're my favourite
Languedoc red wine. You're my rare fillet steak,
You're my squid-ink pasta, you're my *Roquefort*.

Oh, doo de doo, I love to see you walk in from
the university to say hello to me, before I feed us.
The wild cats outside step aside for your passage.
The sporadic weeds hide, the long grass lies down.

Saxophones start up. The paintings on the walls
llght up. All that's missing is the dwarf donkey
to carry your bags. I see him cavorting on the path,
I hear him heehawing. And you stand there laughing.

The Big Umbrella

Aren't you great with your big umbrella?
All the lights are on in the castle.
Why do you talk to me like I'm a horse,
even though I *am* a horse on two legs,
unlike most of the people you've met
tonight or any night. I love your eyes

and your hair, and your smile – every-
thing about you. Who cares if the taxi-
driver spoke Swahili if he got us here.
Do the penguins speak Irish? Yet they
hop around Fota as if they do so.
They're birds, they're not horses.

And no one needs a big blue umbrella
to keep off the rain and the sullen sky.
Oh, let us walk in the rain and get wet,
wetter than fish, then leap in the bowl
where the goldfish flounces around
as if there's no point to anything at all.

The Archery Lesson

I arranged the archery lesson
for eleven, and sure enough
the coach arrived on time at
the *Terraza de los Pajaros*,
bearing two great bows and a
quiver of pointed arrows.

He set up a target – a blue,
cork dog – ten metres away,
showed me the correct stance
and angle of torso to target,
took one bow, fired an arrow
into the dog's belly, and smiled,

handing me the other bow.
I looked around. A couple sat
at a table, sipping Cava.
Maybe they should move.
I boinged the string, needing
more force than I'd anticipated.

He handed me the first arrow.
It was red. I aimed at the dog,
fired. The arrow clattered off
a fortunately empty table. I
tried again with a yellow arrow
which whizzed past the dog's tail.

After an hour I was proficient.
The dog was a multicolour hedge-
hog. I looked around for real dogs
and lemons to put on their heads.
I even glanced at the *pajaros*,
flapping about, but ruled these out.

Lesson over, I signed it to my room,
watched my coach walk away,
swinging his black locks, removing
my bow and my arrows. Time
to visit the internet, I thought, to
fire a bolt with the credit card.

San Francisco

1

A beggar came up to me
on Sutter, pushing a
supermarket trolley
with a large cardboard
box inside it, and in
that, a small dog who
asked me for money –
he sounded drunk.

2

The cable car stuck
on top of a hill –
we all got out and
watched it clank off,
bell ringing, empty.

3

In the market, I ordered
Hog Island Sweetwater
Oysters, small, sweet
fellows who fled into
my mouth, chased by a
Mendocino Pinot Gris.

4

That evening, in the
Sushi bar, the chef
drank sake, and danced
around, shouting,
while his knife sliced
the tuna by itself.

5

In Haight Ashbury
the hippies were gone,
but psychedelic colours
adorned the walls, tarot
readings were offered,
and a woman sat, topless,
on a bench. I smelled
marijuana, and had to lie
down because I was high.

6

While eating dim sum
a transsexual with long
orange hair paused at
the window to give me
the eye. I hid behind
the bamboo and cacti
in the window boxes.

7

I'm looking everywhere
for Blaze, the missing
service dog – he's black
and white, and small.
I need the reward.
Where can he be? Is that
him on the television?

8

The new receptionist
in the hotel is bald,
but has a waxed, pointy
moustache, so sharp it
stabbed me in the cheek
as I side-stepped him.

9

Getting a lift to West
Portal, just after Goat
Hill Pizza, a white van
whizzed past, with
Grateful Dogs Rescue
on it. Had it Blaze?

10

Heading back, I met
a homeless woman
who went on about
the Rapture, how every
day she's waiting to be
lifted up to Heaven.

11

A sign in a shop:
No dog
No food
No bag
No refund
No exchange
No videos
    Thank you.

What *was* allowed?

12

On Van Ness I knew
the waitress in the bar
was a vampire, when
she claimed the bats on
her tights were hearts.

13

On Mission I hovered
outside the sports shop
offering boxing lessons –
I was in need of some
form of self-defence.

14

How did the waiter
In the Italian restaurant
who looked like the
Irish Football Manager
know I was Irish?

15

Trying to escape from
Sutter, no taxi would stop.
An old woman came over
and said she'd got one
for a friend by holding up
a finger and showing
a bit of leg. I tried that.
No joy. There was no
way out of here.

Trainsong

The lambs in the fields are drinking milk.
The trees are enjoying the lack of wind.
A horse splashes through a rainwater pond.
The cows stand in a black & white group.
A door is nakedly open in the red barn.
Two tractors are parked by gravel hills.

Would they drive up those gravel hills?
How long can the mama sheep give milk?
Have lovers had trysts in the red barn?
Has anyone tapped the energy of the wind?
How many times in a day do cows group,
and do they ever flop down in a pond?

They would make a big splash in the pond.
The tractors would sink in the gravel hills.
The Cows would be a great name for a group.
Their debut album could be called *Milk*.
The launch gig could be in the red barn.
They could drown out the howling wind.

How many trees lose branches in a wind?
How many branches fall into the pond?
I see a fire being started in the red barn –
its smoke rises in circles above the hills.
People run at it, throwing buckets of milk.
It works – they are a successful group.

What is the collective name for a group
of snowmen? They wouldn't mind the wind.
They'd approve of the colour of milk.
They wouldn't have much time for the pond.
They could be exhibited in a chilled red barn –
photos could be beamed onto the hills.

Wild horses love galloping over the hills.
When they do so they stay in a group.
On cold nights they sleep in the red barn,
they enter the door to escape the wind.
Outside, the chilly air freezes the pond.
The surface of it begins to resemble milk.

Green Sky

Up in the hills the jackals are howling.
The vultures swoop low overhead.
A yellow parrot lands at my feet
and cackles: 'They want you dead.'

'Let them,' I shout back at him.
'Tell them I'm going nowhere, except
up some steps to pick up a cheque
it will kill them to watch me accept.

The sky can go green for all I care.
Orchids can float by on the breeze.
Donkeys can swim across the Channel.
Artists can loose red dye into the seas,

but I won't sit here to be puked upon.
I'm heading for the deserts of the Moon.
I'll take with me six crows' feathers.
I'm sorry to change my mind so soon.'

The Gare du Nord

The goddesses above the entrance
to the Gare du Nord gaze down
on the three blue-clad policewomen
who stalk the parked cars, searching
for those who are illegally there,
and they find plenty, so all three
make a note of the number, even
when the driver leaps up from a terrace-
table to remonstrate, whereupon
they finger their holstered batons,
as above, one goddess holds a sword,
one a stake, a third a battleaxe –
the heavenly back-up brigade. Taxis
take off and arrive, or sit there,
avoiding the bus-stops, and an open
tour bus crawls past the station.
Then here they are again, the three
ladies in their peaked caps and boots,
and one is on her walkie-talkie, reporting
a new victim whose number is noted,
and whose driver runs out from the café
to protest in vain. No, these three
are never defeated or disappointed –
once a number goes down, it's down,
as the hands slowly move on the clock
above the goddesses who look poised
to jump, then brandish a stake,
a sword, a battleaxe at the miscreant,
behind the three raised batons,
till he pays his fine and runs away.

The Chocolate Mine

They're hacking away in the chocolate-
mine beneath la Madeleine, and soon
their dark wares will go on sale.

They discovered it during a foundation
check. They didn't believe it first, till
the bishop pronounced it a miracle,

and turned the monks into miners
who toil around the clock, amassing
warehouses of pure black stuff.

There's enough to last a year or more,
the Vatican assessor opined, helping
himself to a lorryload he'd share

with the Pope who'd have to come
to inspect it himself, and say a mass to
announce the Holy Chocolate worldwide,

the signal to open the sacred kiosk
inside the entrance of La Madeleine,
to the left, well back from the candles.

This would be staffed by black nuns
who'd speak of the parallel with that
water that was turned into wine

and would oversee the wicker baskets
filling with banknotes in all currencies
while beaming monks looked on.

A week would generate enough income
to solve the wheelchair-access problem,
and polish the huge bronze doors.

In a year, the cardinals would wonder
what they did before the chocolate mine,
what they'd do when it ran out.

The Dead Zone

So soon?, she said, as he stood there
in front of the door, holding a paddle –
one from their forgotten canoe up
in the attic. How come he had it? Was he
a lurker in the floors and corridors of
the house? Had he the power of being
invisible, and slinking upstairs, unseen,
to drag stuff out of that dead zone?

Yeah, a weird music had been playing,
redolent of fairy folk, and he'd been
smaller than a jockey, or a rower in a
barque, but he'd jumped up onto the balcony
singing a madrigal, with no music, except
that of bees pursuing their honey, jars
of which stood piled up in the kitchen,
where he chimed out the whole story.

The Visited Man

(for David O'Meara)

Around his feet
danced a fairy band –
there were five women
and five men,
and none was more than
a few inches high.

All wore red
with touches of gold.
A dog would have barked
them out of the room
but his dog was dead
for over a year.

If he bent down
and tried to stop them
they'd dance right through
his held-out hand
as if they were creatures
of smoke or wind.

They never sang
or they never spoke.
They never looked up
or ceased their dance
till the hands of the clock
crossed at twelve.

Then they filed out
through the door
and he was alone
once more, but he knew
that tomorrow
they'd dance here again.

The Dog and the Moon

The dog tried to bite the moon
but he couldn't jump high enough,
and fell into the river, where
the moon's reflection bobbed.
He couldn't bite this either, so
he swam to the bank, where he
clambered out and ran off, howling,
dripping, to a hole he'd pawed
from a grave, and he lay in there.
But the moon shone down on him
and he gurned, he lashed out,
but his nails caught nothing, so
he rose to his feet and scarpered
through the streets, barking,
scattering people, while the moon
poured its light on him, and he
felt scared in the glow that wouldn't
go away, that brightened, eeried,
until he threw his head back and
unleashed a shrieky crescendo –
barks, howls, whimpers – which
made the moon at least one half-
times bigger, and intensified
its light, making him jump up to
try to bite it again, and fail again.

Broken Flower

A cat is sitting in the tree.
A man is lying on the road
clutching a broken flower.
Crows circle in the sky.
All the wine is in the barn.
All the weather knows is rain,

rain, rain and more rain.
The cat is soaked in the tree.
The wine is dry in the barn.
A bus trundles down the road,
beep follows beep into the sky.
The man gets up with his flower.

The man chucks away his flower,
holds his face up in the rain,
extends his arms to the sky,
goes to piss against the tree,
tries to stagger to the barn,
falls down again on the road.

Cheek pressed against the road,
he thinks about his flower,
about the wine in the barn.
He struggles up in the rain.
The cat jumps from the tree.
A crow caws from the sky.

A watery sun appears in the sky.
The man wobbles down the road,
stopping to lean on the tree,
looking around for his flower.
He doesn't notice there's no rain.
He makes it to the barn.

He's standing there in the barn,
looking back out at the sky,
wondering why there's no rain
bouncing off the road,
why he can't see his flower,
only that stupid tree.

That tree that thrives in the rain.
That road that leads from the barn
to his flower, under a grey sky

Muskerry Villas: A Diptych

1 *The Pigeons' Zone*

The pigeons are going mad today.
They swoop in a great crowd
low over the rooftops, they almost
blast through my window,
they land as one on the mossy
slates and mill around in the sun,
some flapping up to the tiled rim,
one taking roost on the chimney.
What has agitated them, and what
are they now sitting, waiting for?
A second flies up to the chimney
to poke the first awake. Another
turns round and round and round,
then sits down. One advances far
to the left to preen himself, alone,
then hops up onto another chimney.
Nothing is going to arrive unseen.
None of them sit on the skylight
that shit has streaked, and no one
looks up through anymore. This
is the pigeons' zone and I'm a spy.

2 *The Weeds*

The weeds sway in the wind.
They wave their fluffy purple heads
around as if they're creatures
waiting to pounce on something
moving and edible. Their green
leaves are their skin, their brown

stalks are bone. They rear over
the stone wall they've sprung from,
a wall that's losing bits to the air,
to them. No pigeon goes near them,
no person either, though sometimes
a bee floats above them and lands,
and never leaves. They lean out
above the broken slates, as if
sniffing for anything else to snaffle.
The weeds sway in the wind.

Creature Haiku

To skin a tiger
you need a very sharp knife
and superb armour.

To pluck an eagle
you need a crossbow, a sword,
a flash of lightning.

To catch a crayfish
you need a steel net, a fork,
a hipflask of brandy.

To outwit a cobra
you need a bright yellow stick
and a pair of goggles.

To tame a wild horse
you need a lasso, a green
scarf, a soft saddle.

To charm a monkey
you need dazzling teeth, a laugh
that reaches the moon.

To kill a scorpion
you need a bottle of rum
poured into a basin.

Hogs Killing a Snake

(after John Steuart Curry)

The hogs tore the snake
to bits with their teeth.
They tossed it between them.
It writhed and flashed its
fangs, to no avail. They killed
it, then trotted off through
the evergreen forest. The
snake-corpse lay on the
foliage, attracting a pair of
rats, who nibbled at it,
finding the tough skin a
barrier, but they didn't give
up, until a dog arrived,
barking, among the trees,
sending the rats scarpering,
squealing, and a monk with
rosary beads sailed onto
the scene, blessed the snake,
which quivered, shook itself
into action, and slithered away
through the evergreen forest.

The Gallows

We'd hang sixty a day – different heights
for different crimes, thieves at the bottom,
murderers on top, and some would hang
for days, some for months, some for years
(the record was three plus...) till legs, arms
fell off, and the stench, the stench was
caught all over Paris, till those arms, legs
were shovelled into a pit where dogs, cats
waited... You're asking how we decided
how long they'd hang? We didn't. The King
did, and when, inevitably, his own turn came
he didn't hang. He got *madame* instead.

The Loop

I keep going to funerals these days.
Everyone is dying. I'm sick of coffins –
being shouldered by big men, or
sat there at the front of the church
with a candle behind and a wreath
on top. I hate their silver handles.
I hate also the way the priest hijacks
the occasion – transmuting the corpse
into a holy person, even if he/she
would rise from the coffin, screaming
if they heard what was being said.
Yet, people keep dying and I end up
in churches, listening to the lies put out
in the name of Christ, a good man,
who'd have been wonderful to know,
who'd have no time for the spun cant
his words have become. And I watch
the altar boys bring forward the holy
water, the incense, and the thurible
for the priest to anoint the coffin, so
it can slip into the hole in the ground
without a worry. Yeah, maybe,
but I'm thinking it can't be that easy.

The Stomp

You were the only one who could do
the stomp with me, my dead sister.

We'd be at a wedding, the couples
dancing, the music would start

to hop and I'd invite you to join me
on the floor, and we'd go punk-mad,

gyrating, arms–flailing, clearing a space
on the dancefloor. And laughing,

shouting. I thought those stomps
would recur forever. I was wrong.

I though others could take your place,
again I was wrong. No one could.

You were a wild thing, a rare thing.
You were a small horse prancing.

My Problem

The dog wagged her tail
outside the window, as I
stared into her one good eye,
wondering if she understood
why she was banished outside
(I didn't), then I decamped
to the yellow kitchen, where
red flowers spread out of a vase
like the five points of a star
(though scruffier), and I read
poems and listened to jazz,
wishing I could fly, but
the ground is everywhere, and
gravity commands (unfortunately),
and a spider rules the bathroom,
a large red fellow, clearly
a potential pet, whose hairy legs
might provide a logo for the tee-
shirt that could solve the problem
(my problem) of living.

I Don't Want to Get Old

Let me make this clear, I don't want to
get old. I have no desire for loose, wrinkled
skin, or that redness in the face and nose
I see in the couple at the next table,
about to fly off for a week in Jamaica.
I understand, at last, my father's feelings
in his last months, though I don't share yet
his keenness to lie in the grave and sleep
forever. So long in one place sounds terrifying.
What about the music he gave his life to?
I don't imagine it's heard much down there.
And as for the illness that took my mother
away to another world (where the afternoon
before she died, she gave me and the long-
dead Johnny equal time, and didn't know
my sister) I'll pass on that, but I confess
I don't see much to relish in the alternative.
Already my legs are beginning to allow in
peculiar pains, and my hearing admits me to
surrealism. My eyesight, however, is sharp,
plus my hair is the colour it was when I
was that boy who lived on the golf-course,
who played so late he was accused of being
a nocturnal walloper. Is there any chance
at all of becoming that lithe fellow again?

The Sneezer

A sneeze cut the night in half,
as I walked back from the hotel,
whistling an old Dylan tune,
and poking a finger at the stars.

Then fast footsteps followed me,
accompanied by loud exhalations
of breath, till a tall, fat fellow
paced alongside me, laughing

at how he'd caught up with me,
without my running on ahead.
He could be a mugger, he hissed,
then a big sneeze came again.

He then pronounced my name,
and proffered his hand. Startled,
I shook it. I did not know him,
but indeed he seemed familiar –

or almost familiar. Another life,
maybe. His voice had no accent,
or none I could specify. His face
was small for his shape and size.

The moon was round and afloat,
the rain was out on the islands,
so I quickened my pace,
which was no problem to him.

He sneezed once more. The hay,
he muttered, laughing, then he
grabbed my arm. Would you, he
said, accompany me to the sea?

The Ghost

can go through walls, if he wants to
but he does it seldom. He prefers
to adhere to the limits he had before,
as he'd like to be alive again, playing
golf at Ballyliffin, making love to his
girlfriend, cooking *choucroute* with
roast, pre-marinated, loin of pork,
and opening a *Côtes du Rhône Villages*.
But the mountains will fall in the sea
before that can happen, so he drifts
about over the heads of the people
he cared for, occasionally letting them
glimpse him but not be sure they did.

Sometimes he releases a faint, garlic
smell, other times he emits an almost
musical hum, although he could never
sing. Contrary to hearsay, he favours
the day over the night, as the moon
gives him the creeps, even now, while
the sun reminds him of bodily warmth.
Body...! What he'd give to get his own
back, the way it was when he was twenty,
but what has he to give? A spurious aura
that no one believes in? Anyway, he's
here and he's not here, and he knows
he's not wanted but he's staying on.

Co-Author

(i.m. John Hartley Williams)

1

I want to drink a bottle of Petrus
with you. It will cost a thousand euro
or so, but what the hell? Only you
would appreciate it, and with it, maybe,
a small section of that true Roquefort
you once found in the tunnels there
when you went wandering and were
rescued by the cheesemaker's wife
and brought in to taste the real stuff.
I know you told me one time to keep
the food and wine out of the poems
but, man, I connected with you on
that front, and when I come to France
I see you driving here to fill your boot
with bottles of Burgundy for your cellar.

2

Why Petrus? It isn't a Burgundy, but
it's better. The colour is dark, the nose
is truffle and black cherry – not far from
those extravagant poems of yours,
which weren't to everyone's taste,
and were all the better for that.
They used the word 'maverick' for you,
which they do when they don't know
how to place a poet, and the surprises
in your lines still leave them gasping.
Why don't you come back to me as a
unicorn, and invite me to hop on your
back and steer you with my heels to
gallop towards a frothy harbour where
you can jump in, and terrorise swimmers?

3

I emailed you, the night you died,
without knowing that, and got no reply,
of course, but now I want to write
to you again to tell you I can't stand
being in this crap poetry world without
you. We both knew what it was like,
that's why we wrote the book they
hated us for. Yeah, but listen to this –
why don't we shake that world
a bit more, why don't you come back
as a giant white meercat, dressed up
in a tweed suit, and tootling on
a tin whistle, pedal a unicycle
across Trafalgar Square, then jump off
to climb up and hug one of the lions?

4

No, better, come back as that polar bear
who visited you in Grasmere, and
livened up your dull time there.
He was an unruly guest, you said, and
wrecked your joint, but get this,
you can be even more unruly – fling
my computer out the window, eat my
signed first editions, except your own,
roar like an iceberg crashing down.
I read your last stormy poem at your
grave, or what passed for it, with a
bit of a rant about you and English
poetry today. As if it could matter
to you now – it might have one time,
but I'd never have said it back then.

5

Do you remember how much you
laughed when we tried to escape
the Arvon Centre by the back field
to skedaddle to the Half Moon Inn
in Sheepwash for a beer or two,
but were delayed by my plunging
a cream tennis shoe into a cowpat?
It was tempting to see you as a large
monkey then, falling about in mirth,
so why not adopt the form of one?
When we went back to the Centre,
a woman cooked mushrooms she'd
found in the forest and you declined.
Being used to forest life, as a simian,
you would have no problem this time.

6

Oh, where can I go to hear John
Hartley Williams sit at the piano and
pound out ragtime after we've argued
all day? I accused you once of being
the co-author from hell but you
turned out to be far from that.
No, you rewrote the whole novel
in a mad way, but in time I saw
you'd improved it, and we met
in a hotel in central Berlin for six
hours till we agreed on every word.
Only then did we order two beers.
You might have been a crocodile
pretending to play along, before you
gobbled me, but you left me unscathed.

7

I'm up in Donegal, where you never
visited, for whatever reason, and I've
eaten lambchops, grilled pink,
remembering that lunch we had in
your little Greek place by Savignyplatz
where the chef refused to let my lamb
come to the table pink, because no one
in Greece liked it like that. You laughed
but basically agreed with him, even
though I knew you'd been a wolf who'd
roamed the hills of Crete devouring
deer, and any time you cooked meat
for me it came the other side of pink.
You can become that wolf again
and I'll bring you to all my readings.

8

After my life turned upside down I met
you in Novi Sad, where you'd once lived,
and you took me to the fish restaurant
on Ribarsko Ostrova, the island on the
Danube you once prized enough to put
in your great poem 'Bean Soup', and I
wasn't well, but you looked after me,
accompanying me to the pub called in
Serbian *The Bar the Old Men Go
to Die In*, and I didn't die there, not for
the want of trying, and wasn't old yet,
but we survived the experience of being
there, and I permitted you to drive me
to Budapest from where I could catch
a flight to England, then on to Ireland.

9

Long friend, I'm talking to you here,
although you're gone. I'm remembering
that time in my flat in Wilmersdorf,
after an afternoon of writing, when I
opened a bottle of wine and sat you down
to hear one of Johnny Cash's late albums.
Your favourite track was 'The Mercy Seat',
about the electric chair, which you've
had now, in a way of speaking. Jazz
was your thing but you listened to Johnny
and drove away, back to Jenbacherweg,
on the edge of the Brandenberg Forest
where the Volkspolizei used to patrol,
and later, a mushroom doctor sat in a
hut to check the mushrooms we'd picked.

10

Big man, brother, co-author, friend
I've employed a magician who will bring
you back as the Heine-quoting parrot
in our novel, possibly your favourite
character. You'll have to live with me,
and this time you'll quote your own lines.
You can even compose new poems.
I'll feed you pieces of foie gras, if I can
get it, and I'll leave out bowls of Burgundy
(I don't think the Petrus would be apt).
I'll play your favourite old jazz maestros.
And don't worry, there won't be a cage –
you'll have the run of the house in
Sunday's Well, where I cooked for you,
and where we had good times together

Matthew Sweeney was born in Lifford, Co. Donegal, Ireland in 1952. He moved to London in 1973 and studied at the Polytechnic of North London and the University of Freiburg. After living in Berlin and Timişoara for some years, he returned to Ireland and now lives in Cork.

His poetry collections include: *A Dream of Maps* (Raven Arts Press, 1981); *A Round House* (1983) and *The Lame Waltzer* (1985) from Allison & Busby / Raven Arts Press; *Blue Shoes* (1989) and *Cacti* (1992) from Secker & Warburg; *The Bridal Suite* (1997), *A Smell of Fish* (2000), *Selected Poems* (2002), *Sanctuary* (2004) and *Black Moon* (2007) from Jonathan Cape; *The Night Post: A Selection* (Salt, 2010); and *Horse Music* (2013) and *Inquisition Lane* (2015) from Bloodaxe. *Horse Music* won the inaugural Pigott Poetry Prize in association with Listowel Writers' Week, and was a Poetry Book Society Recommendation. *Black Moon* was shortlisted for the T.S. Eliot Prize and for the *Irish Times* Poetry Now Award. He has also published editions of selected poems in Canada (*Picnic on Ice*, Vehicule Press, 2002) and in Germany (*Rosa Milch*, bilingual tr. Jan Wagner, Berlin Verlag, 2008); and two small publications, *The Gomera Notebook* from Shoestring Press, and *Twentyone Men and a Ghost* from The Poetry Business, both in 2014.

He won a Cholmondeley Award in 1987 and an Arts Council Writers' Award in 1999. He has also published poetry for children, with collections including *The Flying Spring Onion* (1992), *Fatso in the Red Suit* (1995) and *Up on the Roof: New and Selected Poems* (2001). His novels for children include *The Snow Vulture* (1992) and *Fox* (2002). He edited *The New Faber Book of Children's Poems* (2003) and *Walter De la Mare: Poems* (2006) for Faber; co-edited *Emergency Kit: Poems for Strange Times* (Faber, 1996) with Jo Shapcott; and co-wrote *Writing Poetry* (Teach Yourself series, Hodder, 1997) and the novel *Death Comes for the Poets* (Muswell Press, 2012) with John Hartley Williams.

Matthew Sweeney has held residencies at the University of East Anglia and the South Bank Centre in London. He was Poet in Residence at the National Library for the Blind as part of the Poetry Places scheme run by the Poetry Society in London, and writer-in-residence at University College Cork. He is a member of Aosdána.